MOMMY COULDN'T FIND HER EYELASHES

Forty-Four Years in First Grade

Mommy COULDN'T FIND HER EYELASHES

MARY JANE FIZER

iUniverse, Inc.
Bloomington

Mommy Couldn't Find Her Eyelashes
Forty-Four Years in First Grade

iUniverse books may be ordered through booksellers or by contacting:

iUniverse
1663 Liberty Drive
Bloomington, IN 47403
www.iuniverse.com
1-800-Authors (1-800-288-4677)

ISBN: 978-1-4759-8139-1 (sc)
ISBN: 978-1-4759-8140-7 (hc)
ISBN: 978-1-4759-8141-4 (e)

Library of Congress Control Number: 2013904302

Printed in the United States of America

iUniverse rev. date: 03/12/2013

DEDICATION

I wish to dedicate this book to all the wonderful first graders—my "Super Kids," whom I have taught over all these years—and to the teachers and other coworkers of mine who encouraged me to write a book. I also wish to dedicate this book to my wonderful family who kept me motivated as I started the book: to my grandchildren, Rylie and Olivia, and their mother, Tina, who made the illustrations for the book; to my daughter-in-law, Queta, who helped me format and input the book into the computer; and to the rest of my family for their patience and understanding as I spent many hours working on this project.

CHAPTER 1

I'm Helping My Mom Learn to Read

I always got so excited when a child began to read fluently, especially one who had struggled to master the concepts of reading. It was such a pleasure to see the joy on a child's face when he or she read a selection fluently for the first time.

A child from Croatia became a very good reader during the course of the school year. I commented on how much progress he had made and how proud I was of him. I asked if his mom helped him in the evenings, and he said, "No, I teach her to read while I am practicing my reading." And he really *was* teaching her how to read!

One day I had a reading group sitting around me on the floor, since our reading table was in use. After they had sat for a few minutes, they began to lie down on the floor to read, which was all right. Then a terrible smell arose, and one child asked who made that smell. Of course, no one accepted the blame, so he proceeded to go from one child to the next, as they lay on their stomachs on the floor, and sniff their bottoms to find out who was the culprit!

CHAPTER 2

How Do You Spell ...?

One day, some of the children were having difficulty learning their spelling words and were not trying to figure out the correct spelling by themselves; they wanted me to spell for them.

One girl, Joanie, spoke up. She said, "You can spell anything you want to if you just sound it out."

Sarah said, "I bet you can't spell 'supercalifragilisticexpialidocious.'"

So Joanie proceeded to go to the chalkboard and, syllable by syllable, she wrote out the word with only one mistake, to the amazement of the entire class—and the teacher!

One of my students, who usually got all the words correct on the weekly spelling test, missed nine out of ten words one week. All the words were from the same word family, so they all ended with the same two letters, but there was no logic to the combinations of letters he had written for each word after the first one, which was correct.

Upon receiving the test paper at home, his mother sent a note to me that said that she couldn't understand what had happened; he knew all the words when he left home that morning.

I called him aside, showed him the test paper that his mom had returned, and asked him if he could tell me why he got so many wrong. Without any hesitation, he said, "When I was in kindergarten, my teacher taught me so much that my brain is so full that if I put anything else in it, it will explode!"

CHAPTER 3

What Goes at the End of a Sentence?

For many years, my students had to respond to a writing prompt in their journals each day and then share what they wrote with the class. Here are some of their more interesting responses to their prompts.

One day, the writing prompt was, "Why do birds fly south for the winter?"

One response was, "Because it is too far to walk, and because they would freeze their butts off if they didn't."

Freddie was sharing his story and had trouble remembering what he had written, so I proceeded to read it for him. He said, "Mrs. Fizer, you are stealing my story!"

One year, when children were writing their stories, they were required to conclude their stories with a sentence that told about how they felt about what they had written. Joey wrote, "I feel happy. I am finished with this story."

After spring break, the class was writing about what they had done on their break. One child wrote, using his own inventive spelling, "On vacation, I was in the water. An it was fun I let a toot in the water. An it felt dum. I laughed. An then we went home."

Another story with inventive spelling was, "I like the Easter Bunny Becus He Brne us candy. I like Easter Sunday cus Jesuse rosis from the ded."

Billy always forgot to put periods at the end of sentences. A teaching assistant in my classroom was reviewing what he had written and asked him what he should put at the end of the sentence that had no punctuation there. He responded, "A pyramid?"

One spring, we were doing a lesson about alphabetical order. The students had to complete a worksheet that had a list of vegetables to be put in alphabetical order. The children had to write the names of the vegetables, in alphabetical order, on the packets pictured on the worksheet and then draw a picture of each vegetable on its packet. We discussed the names of the vegetables and talked about what the unfamiliar ones, like eggplant, looked like, before they started their work. It was interesting to hear the discussion taking place at one table, where a girl and boy from Ghana, a boy from Peru, a boy from Guatemala, and a local boy were working. They were having a discussion of what kind of beans they would draw.

Earlier, when we had discussed the various vegetables, I had pictured green beans in my mind.

The Peruvian child said he would make black beans, the Guatemalan was going to make red beans, and the American was going to make green beans. One of the boys said, "You know, if you plant the little beans in the ground, they will grow and make more beans."

The girl from Ghana got very excited and said, "I am going to make jelly beans, and I will plant some jelly beans when I get home so I can have a lot more jelly beans!"

The American boy said, "You can't plant jelly beans. If you do, they will rust in the ground!"

CHAPTER 4

How Much Is 5 + 5?

ath was always one of my favorite subjects to teach. There are so many different ways to help the children master the basics.

One thing that the students always enjoyed was a math relay. They would divide into teams, and the first child in line on each team would go to the chalkboard to write the answer to the problem that I wrote on the board.

One day during one of these relays, Gina, who had a lot of difficulty with math concepts, was at the board and, instead of trying to figure out what 5 + 5 equaled, she asked me to tell her the answer so that her team could get the point.

I told her that I couldn't tell her the answer. I said that it would be cheating if I did, to which she replied, "I will pay you if you will tell me."

I insisted that I couldn't tell her the answer, and she said, "Oh, come on, Mrs. Fizer. I will pay you one hundred dollars if you tell me the answer."

Needless to say, I did not tell her, and she did not get the answer correct, because her time was spent trying to bribe me to tell instead of figuring out the answer.

Another day, a child was having trouble solving two-digit addition problems. I asked her why she couldn't do the problems. She said, "Because I don't have sixty-two fingers and this number is sixty-two!"

CHAPTER 5

When I Am One Hundred Years Old, I Will ...

Each year, as part of our math curriculum, we counted days until the hundredth day of school. On that day, we did special things involving one hundred to celebrate the occasion. One of the activities was for the students to write what they thought they would look like when they were a hundred years old. Here are some responses!

"If I am a hundred years old, I would be blind and old. I would have a cane and a dog that can see for me."

"I will look like I am about to die, and I look very, very old, but I'm going to heaven."

"I think I will look like my grandmother."

"I am a hundred years old. I can't walk. I'm bald."

"I will look like Mrs. Fizer."

"If I were a hundred, I will be crazy."

"I will have a big beard. I will have gray hair."

"If I was a hundred years old, I would have to have a cane and a wheelchair, and I will have wrinkles."

"If I was a hundred years old, I would blow up, and I will fly, and I will not do nothing, and I will have a newspaper."

Another assignment was to write a response to the question, "What would you do with a hundred dollars?" Some responses were:

"I will save the hundred dollars, and then I will get more money, and then I will be rich!!!"

"I will buy a hundred chocolate-chip cookies."

"I will save it for the beach."

"I will buy a hundred Nintendo 64 games."

"I would buy a hotel or go to Florida or buy a new sofa or a new house or lots of food or a Jacuzzi or a big hot-air balloon or lots of centers or a big bed or lots of glasses or a lot of TVs or lots of schools or lots of water or get more money or more Band-Aids or lots of computers or markers."

"I will go shopping and will save some for my mom. We will go to school. We will go to see Mrs. Fizer. We will see her house."

As we were discussing different ages of people, one child said, "Anyone who is between thirty and one hundred years old is already dead!"

CHAPTER 6

What Was in Lincoln's Hat?

always enjoyed our social studies classes. I came up with many ways to make the lessons more exciting for the children, sometimes with interesting results.

When we were studying Abraham Lincoln, we would talk about his tall stovepipe hat. I told the children that he had a secret pocket inside his hat and asked what they thought he would carry in the pocket. The first reply was, "Rabbits!"

Each year, the first-grade classes in our school participate in a Flat Stanley project. Each teacher reads the story about Flat Stanley to the class, and the children discuss how Stanley became flat and was mailed to another state in an envelope.

Then the students each make a Flat Stanley small enough to fit in an envelope and take home a letter to their parents asking them to send back to school the name and address of a relative or friend to whom they would like to mail their Flat Stanley. Each child mails the envelope with his or her Flat Stanley and a letter to the recipient explaining the project. The recipient is asked to show Stanley around town, take pictures, and send Stanley back to the child—along with a picture and letter telling about what he did during his visit.

One of my students was from Vietnam and had just returned from visiting her grandmother there, so I said that it would really be great if we could get a letter from her grandmother in Vietnam. The next day, as the students arrived and were handing me their addresses, this particular child handed me an envelope that was addressed to her grandmother. She said that her parents did not know how to make a dress. I was confused about this until I looked inside the envelope and found a paper dress that she had cut out and colored, as well as a paper doll that she had cut out and colored to put the dress on. She said that she hoped that this dress was all right; she wasn't sure how to make *a dress*!

As the letters came back to school, we marked where letters came from for each class on a graph that we drew on a hallway bulletin board. It was always interesting to see how many different states and countries were represented. Often, people sent gifts along with the letters. For example, one student in my class received a T-shirt for each classmate with the name of the state on the front!

During career month, parents are invited to share what they do at their jobs with the children. One morning, the guidance counselor appeared in my room and asked if we would like to see a presenter at ten o'clock. I replied that we would be happy to see him.

One of the students asked, "We are going to see a prisoner at ten o'clock?"

While we are studying careers, I have the children write about what they want to be when they grow up. Here are some of their stories.

"I want to be either the president or a forklift operator." (This student is now a teacher!)

"I want to be either a garbage collector or a teacher."

"I want to be a nurse so I can help people who are dead."

CHAPTER 7

I Think I Have Head Lights!

A boy in my class who had allergies to nuts came up to me in the cafeteria one day, very concerned because he couldn't find his lunch. We went back to the classroom to look for it, and it was nowhere to be found. So I took him to the nurse, who knew just what he could and could not eat, hoping that she could help him select something from the cafeteria menu that day that he could eat. She checked the menu and found two or three things that he could have and told him to get those from the cooks. He replied, "But my lunch is in the cafeteria. I only lost my container of cookies."

Each year we are required to watch a video, mostly in cartoon form, about head lice. Toward the end of the video, a real person comes on the screen and tells the children that, if they have an itchy head, they should see the school nurse, who will check to see if they have head lice. At the end of the video, one of the boys came to me and said, "Mrs. Fizer, I need to go to see the nurse. My head is itching. I think I have head lights."

At the end of the school year, my class had an assignment to write a thank-you letter to the school nurse. One letter said, "Dear Mrs. Jacoby, Thank you for the nose bleed."

Early in the school year, we had our annual tornado drill. I explained ahead of time that it was just a practice drill and that it was very important that we do it correctly in case we should ever have a real tornado. I said that the children were to get into their positions (which we demonstrated) in the hallway and were not to talk or giggle so they could hear any instructions that may be given.

I was so proud of my class for following the directions and being very quiet until the drill was almost over, when I could hear a faint voice saying, "Mrs. Fizer, Mrs. Fizer." I walked up and down the line of children to identify who was talking and found Felix with his head in a pool of blood. His nose had started to bleed. I asked him why he didn't tell me earlier, and he said, "You told us that we couldn't talk or move." So when we returned to the classroom, we talked about when it is acceptable to break a rule and talk!

CHAPTER 8

It Isn't Allowed to Snow!

As we were discussing the weather one day in January, Julie stated that she had heard the weatherman say that snow was predicted for that day. Kenny replied, "It will not snow today. It is not allowed to snow after Christmas!"

In one of my earlier years of teaching, we were studying electricity, and I was explaining how an electrical circuit works. I set up the experiment that I had done several times in previous years with no problems, making a circuit with a lightbulb, a switch, batteries, wire, and a doorbell. When it was all set up, I asked one of the students to pull the switch to see what would happen. Nothing happened. Another child tried, to no avail.

We tried several times more after I checked all the connections and could see nothing wrong with what I had set up. I told the class that I would check everything again after school and that we would try again the next day.

Then one child, who often did not seem to be paying much attention to what was going on, walked up to me and said, "I know what we can do, Mrs. Fizer. We can pray, and I will pray right now."

Before I could say anything, he closed his eyes, folded his hands under his chin, and proceeded to pray. He was not praying out loud, but his lips were moving. After a minute or two, he asked, "Can I try now?" I, of course, told him that he could, and, lo and behold, when he pulled the switch, the lightbulb lit up and the doorbell rang!" Never underestimate the power of prayer!

What a surprise, one hot summer day, when I heard a knock at the door of my home and opened it to find one of my first graders standing there with a big pumpkin in his hands. He had grown it from a plant that we had started from seeds in the classroom. I had told the students to put the plants in their gardens at home and, if their plants grew, to let me know about it. A good listener, he brought me one of the products of his plant!

Each fall, when the leaves begin to change, I ask the children to bring to school toilet-paper rolls, which we use to make binoculars. We staple two rolls together, punch a hole in each one at one end, and tie yarn onto them to make it possible to hang the binoculars around one's neck. The children then go outside to the trees around the edge of the playground and use their binoculars to look for signs of fall. Much to my surprise, one morning as the children were arriving and giving me their toilet-paper rolls, Terry brought me a four-pack of toilet paper, not empty rolls! He said that his daddy thought that I needed the paper on the rolls. I had him take the toilet paper back home with a note explaining to his dad why I was returning it. The next year, I made certain that I was more specific in my directions, asking for "empty toilet-paper rolls."

CHAPTER 9

I'm Digging Up My Grandfather!

Our county is located just a few miles from Washington, DC, so we are fortunate to have an abundance of places to go for field trips. One day, we had hired charter buses to take us to the Children's Museum. Shortly after we left the school grounds, we passed a yellow school bus going down the street. David called out, "Look, there is a real bus over there!"

Our first-grade classes were scheduled to go on a field trip to a farm one day in May. The day before the trip, heavy rains were forecast for the day of the trip, so we rescheduled the trip for the following week. We sent notes home to the parents, asking those who had agreed to go as chaperones if they could go the next week. As the students arrived the next day, I was checking to see whose parents could still go with us. When Jeremy arrived, I asked him if his mom could still go with us. He replied, "No, Mrs. Fizer, she can't go with us now, because you changed the weather!"

Another time, all of our first-grade classes were at a nearby state park for a picnic on a very hot day just before the end of the school year. The children had participated in several activities and were getting tired. The last activity for my class was a relay race. Maria asked that she be excused from doing the race because she was very hot, so the chaperone for her group told her that she could sit on the sidelines with her and watch. Soon after, Maria picked up a stick and began to dig in the dirt near where she was sitting. She began to dig harder and faster and harder and faster. The chaperone asked why she was digging so hard and she replied, "I am trying to dig up my grandfather! He died, and I miss him and want to see him again!"

CHAPTER 10

Mommy Couldn't Find Her Eyelashes!

t is always very interesting to hear students explain why they were absent from school. Here are some choice explanations. Parents would be appalled to hear some of them!

Adam was absent one day, and the next day, I welcomed him back and told him that we had missed him. I then said, "Were you sick?"

He replied, "No, my mom had to get me ready for school, and then, when we were ready, she couldn't find her purse, so we had to look for it, and then, when she found it, she couldn't bring me to school because she couldn't drive me to school because she couldn't find her eyelashes."

Dante, who was frequently absent, returned to class after being absent for two days. I asked him why he was absent, and he responded, "I was at Foot Locker buying some new shoes."

Samuel, a third grader who had been in my class in first grade and whose brother, Eli, was currently in my class, appeared at my door one morning and said that Eli was not going to be in school that day because he was sick. I told Samuel that we would miss Eli and asked what was wrong with him. Samuel said that he was not supposed to tell me why his brother was sick, but he would anyway. Eli was sick because he was picking his nose and that made him very sick!

I was very seldom absent from school. Usually, if I missed school, it was for a meeting and I knew ahead of time about it, so I would tell the children that I would not be there the next day. However, I was absent one day without telling the children.

The next day, Shelby said, "Mrs. Fizer, I am so glad you are back. I missed you. I was worried about you. I was afraid that you had lost your job and was homeless and living on the streets."

I assured her that I was all right and that I would always thereafter let her know ahead of time if I was going to be absent so she wouldn't have to worry about me!

CHAPTER 11

I Need to See the Nurse

When students do not feel well in school or pretend to feel ill, it is often fun to hear their explanations of why they don't feel well. Here are some choice ones.

Debbie came to me one day with a very sad face, rubbing her arm. I asked her what was wrong, and she said, "My arm hurts so much"

I looked at her arm and felt it and could see nothing wrong, so I said, "I think you may be having growing pains."

She looked at me with a very surprised expression and said, "That's what my mother said too!" She then returned to her desk with no more complaints for the rest of the day.

Brittany came to me, complaining that her eye hurt. I asked her why it was hurting, and she said, "Because I keep sticking my finger in it."

Jared became quite ill just before Christmas and was admitted to Children's Hospital in Washington, DC. It was the custom for the president's wife to visit the hospital during the holidays and read to the children. Jared's mom was keeping me informed of his progress there and told me that he was very excited about getting to meet First Lady Barbara Bush. But, just as he approached her, he threw up—all over her. She was very gracious and said that it was all right, that her children and grandchildren had done the very same thing!

George seemed very upset one day, and I asked him if something was wrong. He replied that he was worried about his dad, who was in the hospital. I asked what was wrong, and he said, "He has nerves."

Willie was missing when we returned from lunch one day. I asked the students where he was, and one of them said that he had vomited in the lunchroom and was sent to the nurse. Willie returned to the classroom a few minutes later to get his belongings so he could go home, and one of the children, who had not seen him get sick, said, "Did you vomit in the cafeteria?" Willie replied, "No, I didn't vomit. I puked."

One day, Ricky said to me, "My butt is hurting." I asked him what he thought could be wrong and he said, "Because I am pinching it."

Sue came up to me near the end of the day holding her head. Very dramatically, she said that she had a headache. I asked her if she knew why her head was hurting, and she said, "I think I learned too much today!"

One year, I had the privilege of having my son, Tim, working with me as my teacher's aide. He developed a great rapport with the children, and they often turned to him with a concern instead of turning to me. One day, we had completed the weekly spelling test, and my son was sitting at my desk grading the papers while I was at the reading table leading a group lesson. The rest of the children were working at their desks when Alice interrupted me at the reading table to say that she did not feel well. Because she frequently complained about not feeling well when she just wanted to go home, I asked her to return to her desk and continue with her work and see how she felt later.

Instead of following these directions, she stopped at my desk and, as she proceeded to tell Tim that she wasn't feeling well, she threw up all over him, the spelling-test papers, and the desk. Startled by this, Tim jumped up and yelled, "Shit!" He immediately looked at me to see my reaction because he knew that I didn't approve of using words like that! He then left to go home to shower and change his clothes. I sent Alice to the nurse, who called her mother to come and pick her up.

CHAPTER 12

My Big Brother Will Catch Me!

On the playground, Ellen, who is a very dramatic young lady, came screaming and crying to me, saying, "Mrs. Fizer, Mrs. Fizer, you've got to help me, Mrs. Fizer. I fell in the mud, and my hair is all muddy. You have to wash my hair for me. I can't look like this all day. Please help me! I can't let anyone see me looking like this!" She didn't look bad at all, just a tiny spot of mud in her hair. She went to the nurse and got the mud out so she felt better. Such dramatics!

Brian was always very well dressed, looking like a miniature high school student. He was very aware of his appearance and frequently called others' attention to how he looked and what he wore. Because of overcrowded conditions that year, classroom trailers had been placed around the edge of the playground near the building. Students were told not to play between the trailers because they might disturb the children working inside. There was also a safety concern, since the supervising teachers couldn't see them. Brian didn't follow these instructions, and one day, he came running to me, very upset, looking as if he had fallen in the mud. He said that he ran behind the trailers to get a ball and slipped and fell, but it was not mud that he fell into, it was dog poop, and he had it all over his face, hands, and beautiful sweater—even in his hair. I had a very hard time keeping from laughing!

On the playground one day, one of my girls, who had her hair in beautiful braids pulled back into a ponytail, came to me with the ponytail in her hand and told me that her hair had fallen out. I am thankful that the ponytail was made of hair extensions! We put them in a baggie and sent them home!

Tommy bumped his head on the bars at recess and came running to me. He was very reluctant to go to the nurse to have his head checked, and, as I walked with him down the hall to the nurse, he explained why: "I am afraid my brains are going to fall out."

Cindy fell off the bars one day at recess time, and she and her friend Eve came to me, both very upset and crying. Eve was afraid that she would get into trouble because she hadn't held on to Cindy and Cindy had fallen.

Cindy said, "Don't worry. I'm not going to tell on you. My big brother is up in heaven and is watching over me, and if I fall, he will spread his big wings and fly down and catch me before I get hurt!"

Our principal was involved in a car accident on an icy road on the way to school one winter day and broke his collarbone. When he was able to return to school, he had his arm in a sling and a sweater to cover the arm for additional protection. One of my boys came in from the bus, very wide-eyed with surprise, and said, "Mrs. Fizer, Mrs. Fizer, have you seen the principal? He is going to have a baby!"

CHAPTER 13

Daddy Didn't Get Me a Dog!

S tudents are constantly sharing with their teachers sad things that have happened or are happening in their lives. Here are some of these sad stories shared with me.

One day, the writing prompt was "One Time When I Felt Sad." Jerry wrote that he was sad because his dog died. The dog had to be put to sleep because he was sick. His dad promised him that he would get him another dog. The conclusion to the story was, "But, Mrs. Fizer, he lied! He didn't get me a dog! He lied!"

Martha, who was new to the community, was very sad at recess on one of the first days of school. I talked with her about what was making her sad, and she said that they had to give their dog away because her big sister wouldn't feed the dog and because another sister was allergic to dogs. I tried to console her by saying that maybe one of her friends might have a dog that she could play with sometimes. She replied that her friend lived far, far away, where they had moved from, and she couldn't go there to play with her. Since she was still sad, I told her that maybe when she became a grown-up, she could have her own house and get her own dog— and she said that her children might be allergic to dogs!

The mother of one of my students was very ill with cancer and passed away in the spring. I called the father to see if there was anything I could do to help, and he replied, "Just be there to hold my son's hand when he needs a hand to hold." I attended the funeral service and was glad to see that his son was doing very well under the circumstances.

Darren went into the restroom in our classroom during math class one day. The students know that, unless it is an emergency, they do not go to the restroom during instruction time. He stayed in the restroom for a long time, and I became concerned about whether he was all right. I knocked on the door and asked him if he was okay. Darren replied that he was. He still didn't come out, though.

Then Annie said that she needed to go to the restroom, so I knocked again and told Darren that he must come out so someone else could use the restroom. He reluctantly came out, and Annie started in and stopped at the door and yelled, "Mrs. Fizer, Mrs. Fizer, you have to come here!"

I imagined that I would see the worst and was greatly surprised at what I did see. Darren had taken the toilet tissue and wrapped it around and around the handicap bars on the sides and back of the restroom, over and over again, making it look like a spider's web. I cannot imagine how he got out without breaking some of the paper, but it was all intact.

I asked him why he did this, and he said that he did not know. I then told him to return immediately to the restroom and clean up all the paper. So he went in again and shut the door and stayed for another long period of time. When he came out, all the paper was rolled very neatly onto the cardboard roll!

I talked with him later about why he had done this, and he still said that he didn't know. I was so concerned about this unusual behavior from a child who was usually so well-behaved that, as soon as school was over, I called his mom to see if she could shed some light on what had occurred. I was very surprised when she told me that he had been very upset that morning when he left for school because his grandfather, whom he was very close to, had passed away, and the funeral was that day. His mom had decided that it would be better for him to be in school than to go to the funeral, which he had wanted to attend. So we figured that this was his way of getting rid of his frustration and grief at not getting to go to the funeral. He never did anything like that again.

CHAPTER 14

I Changed My Birthday!

I always enjoyed celebrating holidays in my classroom. The children always learned a lot about the various holidays while having fun doing activities and projects for each one.

We were celebrating an October birthday in our classroom, and Joey, who had a September birthday and had already had his celebration, came to me and said, "I changed my birthday. It is in October!"

When we were discussing the upcoming Memorial Day holiday, which was on May 27 that year, the twins in my class, who were born on Memorial Day, said that Memorial Day could not be on May 27 because they were born on Memorial

Day and their birthday was May 26. Therefore, Memorial Day had to be May 26 every year!

Toward the end of the school year, I usually have a special day to celebrate the birthdays of those students who have summer birthdays so that they will not feel left out. Then I send those children birthday cards when their birthdays arrive. I had just mailed a card to Donnie when I met him in a store where I was shopping. We talked for a few minutes about what he had been doing since school was out, and then I wished him a happy birthday. He looked very surprised and said, "How did you know it was my birthday?"

I said, "Don't you know that teachers know everything?"

His eyes got huge, his mouth opened wide in surprise, and he ran down the aisle, and I didn't see him again!

CHAPTER 15

How Do You Cook a Turkey?

During November, my students often made an instruction book explaining how to cook a turkey, in their own words. They dictated their ideas to me, I typed them into a booklet, and they illustrated their stories and decorated the covers. Here are some of their ideas on how to cook a turkey.

"I will look in the woods and find a turkey and kill it. When I get home, I will decorate it with flowers and feathers. Then I will put it in the oven for ten minutes. I will show it to my mom and dad and then eat it."

"My granddad and me go hunting and shoot a turkey. We go back home. We skin the turkey. We wash it. We put it in the oven and cook it for twenty minutes. Me and my granddad and grandmom set out the turkey. My cousins come over, and we all eat the dinner."

"First, I would stuff it with meat and take the temperature. I see how many pounds it is. Then I would cook it. I would cut it up. I would break the wishbone. I will save the turkey for next Thanksgiving dinner."

"My mom never cooks a turkey, but I would put macaroni in it and ice cream. I would get some chicken and decorate it with food. Put it in the stove and make it hot. Cook it for six minutes. Take it out and serve it."

"First, put hot dogs and sauce on it. Then put it in the oven. Cook it twenty minutes. Take it out and put it on a big plate. Then cut it. We eat it."

"Take the feathers off. Stuff it with feathers and acorns. Put it in the oven for a half hour. Take it out of the oven. Eat it."

"First, wash the turkey. Stuff it with lots of stuff like mashed potatoes and tomatoes. Cook it for one hour in the oven. Put it on the table. Eat it."

"Kill it first. Pull the skin and thing under its neck off. Cook it two hours. Put sauce inside it. Pull it out of the oven, and put it on a plate. Eat it."

"First, put rubber in the turkey so it can't go away. Then put it in the microwave. Cook it for three minutes. Take it out. Cut it. Eat it."

"I will kill a turkey in the woods. I will bring it home and stuff it with chicken bones. Cook it for two hours. Take it out. Put it on the table. Eat it."

"First, buy a turkey that is dead. Then cut it if it looks big. Then stuff it with flowers and fish. Then I will put it in the oven. Leave it for forty-five minutes. Take it out and eat it. "

"Get a turkey at the farm. I will put something in the turkey's side that won't hurt him but will kill him. Take the feathers off so we won't die when we eat it. Stuff the leaves in the turkey. Cook it in my pan. Cook chicken too. Cook for twenty minutes and take the leaves out. Take out the thing that killed him. Eat it."

"Get a turkey from the jungle. Shoot it. Water it so the blood can come out. Put it in a pot. Cook it for eleven seconds. Put it on the table. When the Pilgrims and Indians come, say, "Happy Thanksgiving!" I will tell them that this is good because I made the real turkey and I have a secret way to make it."

"Get a turkey from the forest. I will shoot it like the Indians with a bow and arrow. Take off the feathers. I will put it in a giant pot. I will cook it one time. Eat it."

"Get the turkey out of the backyard. Kill it and cook it until Thanksgiving Day. Cut the feathers off. When it is done, I'll make some ice cream. I'll put the feathers in the ice cream and serve it on Thanksgiving Day."

"Go hunt for a turkey. My mom will help me chase him around the house. Then we will catch the turkey. My mom will get a knife and cut it up. Take off the feathers and skin. Cook it for ten minutes. Eat it."

"Get a turkey from the woods. Kill it. Wash it. Pick off the feathers. Stuff it with baked beans and corn and apple pie and ice cream. Cook it in the oven for twenty minutes. Eat it."

"Get a turkey at the store. Take everything off of it. Stuff it with circle things and toothpicks. Put some cherries on the toothpicks. Cook it in the oven at 350 for twenty minutes. Eat it."

"Stuff the turkey with a mashed-potato pusher. Put in peppers, and I think it's gotta be brown stuff called nuts and stuffing. Cook it for ten minutes. When ten minutes is up, pull it out and eat it."

"Get a turkey from Giant. Season it with pepper, salt, the stuff you put on deviled eggs. Put it in the oven for ten minutes.

Take it out and let it cool. Once it is cool, take it out of the oven and take it outside. We eat on the deck. Some of our friends come. Our grandmas and grandpas come. Our aunts come too. Our cousins come."

"My mom gets a turkey from Safeway. She sometimes cleans it out. She puts Stove Top stuffing inside. I guess she probably puts it in the oven. When she cooks the turkey, she lets us play outside. Then we come in and get ready to eat the turkey. Then she takes the turkey out and cuts it in half. Then she gets a little bit of turkey for her boyfriend. She saves some turkey for tomorrow. Then we go to bed, and I read a book. Then she brings my sister over, and she gets some turkey and eats it."

"Get a turkey from the store. Take the stuff that is in it out. Put corn and carrots in it. Cook it on the stove for ten minutes. I will call everyone in my family to come to my house and eat dinner. I will cut the turkey open and bake a cake and put doughnuts out and salad, and I might put out macaroni and hot dogs. I will put out hamburger and have a cookout. I will bring ice cream. We will have a picnic at the park."

CHAPTER 16

What Was in Santa's Train?

It was always fun to celebrate Christmas at school, with carol singing, programs, parties, and more. I really missed all this fun when we were no longer allowed to do anything for this holiday. One story stands out from when we could celebrate Christmas.

On a bulletin board in the classroom, I had placed a "Santa Train," and each child made a picture of what he or she wanted most for Christmas. The children told the class about their wishes and then placed their pictures in one of the cars on the train.

Suzy came up to share her picture, which looked like two circles touching each other with lines coming from the top of each circle. Everyone, including me, was very puzzled about her picture—until she explained that she wanted a bra just like her friend had!

One year, just before the winter break, Nathan came to class with a pretty gift bag. He came up to me and said, "This is a present for you. Let me show you what it is!" and proceeded to open the bag and remove the gift from it!

CHAPTER 17

You're a Nice Old Lady!

One of my boys brought me a gift for Valentine's Day and asked for the bag back. He said his mom always wanted him to bring the bag back home!

On one Valentine's Day, I returned to my classroom during my lunch break to find an FTD Federal Express package sitting on my desk. I excitedly opened it to find a beautiful basket of miniature roses and a note that said that it was from Denise, one of my students. When I brought the children back to the classroom after lunch, they saw the flowers on my desk and asked where they came from. I told them how pretty the flowers were and thanked Denise for them. She said, "My mom said that we should send you some flowers for Valentine's Day because you are such a nice *old* lady!"

CHAPTER 18

Mommy Said I Could Pinch!

On the day before St. Patrick's Day, some of the students were excitedly talking about how they were going to pinch anyone who did not wear green the next day. I warned them that, in my class, they were not allowed to pinch anyone. Bobby came in the next day and said, "My mom told me that it is not fair for you not to let us pinch on the seventeenth!"

He was very upset because I still would not let him pinch his friends!

CHAPTER 19

I Don't Like This Punch!

Each year, my students have a Mother's Day tea for their moms. They sing songs, read poems, put on a play, and serve their parents refreshments. They also make tissue-paper corsages for them.

Joshua was having a terrible time getting the paper to separate. I said that I knew he could do it—that he had done the same thing in kindergarten. He replied, "But in kindergarten, the teacher did everything for us."

At one of our annual Mother's Day teas, the children had served punch and cookies to their moms and then gotten their own refreshments. After taking a sip of her punch, Cheryl walked up to the punch bowl, poured her cup of punch back into the bowl, and said, "I don't like this punch!"

CHAPTER 20

My Mom's the Best!

y students make booklets for their moms telling them why they are special. Here are some of their ideas about special moms.

"My mom is special because she helps me pack my lunch. She helps me hang up my jacket. She loves me because I help her a lot."

"My mom is special because she just is. She pays for our house."

"My sister is the best sister because she is very nice to me and she lets me go places with her. I'm writing about my sister because my mom died. My sister takes care of me."

"My mom is the best mom because she loves me, and she spends lots of time with me. If I need help with my homework, she will help me do it. Also, I think my mom is the best mom in the world. If she's late at my babysitter's, she will take me to Safeway to get a doughnut."

"My mom is the best mom of all. She is the best because she watches over me. She helps me when I need help, and she draws with me. She plays with me. We play hide-and-seek. I like my mom because she feeds me. She dresses me. She makes my bed. We go to the movie theater. We play music, and we exercise. We do art. We read together. I feel very, very, very happy."

"My mom is the best mom of all. She is the best because she gets a lot of money. She is also the best because she buys me stuff. I like my mom because she cooks good, and I help her cook. I love my mommy."

"My mom is the best mom of all. She is the best because she is my mother. She also is the best because she loves me and I love her. I like my mom. She makes me happy. I love my mom because we spend time together. She makes me feel special!"

"My mom is the best mom of all. She is the best because she makes the best, best food. She is also the best because she is very, very, very nice. I like my mom because she teaches me a lot. She loves me a lot. I also like my mom because she cares for me and teaches me times and divide. I also like my mom because she is good to me. She is also the best because she teaches me new things. She is also the best because she helps me with my homework. I also like my mom because she helps me get ready for school and helps with everything I want to do. She also teaches lots of good things and does not teach me bad things. She is the best."

"My mom is the best mom of all. She is the best because she is nice to me. She is also the best because she keeps me protected. I like my mom because she'll never let anyone hurt me. I also like her because she helps me. I love you, Mom! I feel happy!"

"My mom is the best mom because she lets me play with my friends after I do my homework. Sometimes when she has money, she lets me ask my friends to go out to eat with us. She lets me ask my friends to sleep over on my birthday and lets us go outside at dark and tell scary stories."

"My mom is the best mom of all. She is the best because she is really nice. She is also the best because she takes care of me. I like my mom because she helps me do my homework and plays with me. She washes my clothes. She washes the dishes. She bakes cookies with me. I love my mom, and she is the best mom I can ever have. That makes me happy."

"My mom is the best of all. She is the best because she loves me very, very much. She is also the best because she cares for me and because she pays attention and because we play games like Uno. She is very funny, and she sings well. I like my mom because she works hard and gets money, and with the money she buys me stuff. She always tells me the truth. She lets me have sleepovers. On Saturdays, she lets me stay up late, and I like that. She takes time to listen to me. I think she is sweet. I would not trade my mom even if I met a girl just as nice, so now you see why she's the perfect mom. I think that because she is the best mom in the world. She is so trustworthy. I can always trust her."

"My mom is the best mom because she takes me to the mall and we buy teenager clothes for me. She is also the best because she lets me do whatever I want. Sometimes she lets me pick what day care I want to go to. Sometimes she is not cool. She makes me feel cool."

CHAPTER 21

This Is How to Cook!

We also have made cookbooks for our moms for Mother's Day. Here are some of the students' original recipes.

Chicken

Take flour, salt, and pepper. Put it in a bag and mix it up. Then put chicken in it. Shake it up. Take the chicken out, and fry it in real hot grease.

Put butter and onion inside the chicken. Then take out the onion. Cook it in the oven.

Cut up the chicken. Put flour on it. Then you cook it in oil. Take it out of the pan. Put it in a bowl. Eat it.

Macaroni and Cheese

Put noodles in a pan of hot water. Turn on the thing so it can boil. Then after it is done, put it in the thing with holes in the sink. When it is done, put in the cheese. Mix it. That's all.

Cook the macaroni. Put butter in it. Put the cheese that comes inside the box with it. Then put in some pepper, and I'm not sure about salt, and milk. Then stir it up. Eat it!

Go to the store. Get a box of macaroni and cheese. Then go home and put the macaroni in a pot. Then put in the magic sauce. Then put it on the oven to cook.

Get a big pan, and put boiling water in it. Put in a whole box of macaroni. Wait for ten minutes; then put in the cheese and some extra cheese. Put a teaspoon of salt in. Sprinkle on some pepper.

Pizza

Get some cheese and a square pan. Put stuff in the bottom of the pan like when you make cupcakes. Put peppers and pepperoni and cheese on. Cook in the oven.

Spaghetti

First, you take a box of spaghetti—my mom uses seven boxes of spaghetti sticks. Then take some tomatoes in a can, sort of like sauce. Then take a great big pot of hot boiled water. Then put the boxes of spaghetti in the pan. Cook them in the pan. That's all.

Baked Potatoes
First, you get a baked potato. Wash the skin off. Then you put it in the oven for an hour to a half an hour. Then get it out, put it on a plate, cut it up, and put butter on it.

Bologna Sandwich
First, take two pieces of bread. Then you take mayonnaise and put it on the two pieces of bread. Then you put lettuce and then bologna. Then you take the other piece of bread onto the bologna, and then it is all done.

Peanut Butter and Marshmallow Sandwiches
You need two pieces of bread. Then you need marshmallow crème. Then you need peanut butter. Then you need to spread peanut butter on one piece of bread. Then spread marshmallow crème on the other piece. Put the two pieces together. Then you eat it.

Apple Cider
First cut up apples. Put in sugar. Boil it. Take it off the stove.

Angel Food Cake
Get some white cake mix. Then mix it up. Then stick it in the oven. Wait for about sixty or eighty minutes. Take it out of the oven.

Peanut Butter Cookies
Put eggs and some peanut butter in a bowl. Stir it around. Put it in the oven, and let it cook. Take it out. Make some more.

Banana Bread

Take three bananas, and put them in a bowl or food processor, and smash them up. I think you put two eggs in. Take some butter, melted, and put it in a pan. Put it in the bowl. Take 3 ½ cups of whole-wheat flour and 3 ¼ spoons of baking soda. Put it in one of those little meatloaf things. Then you wait for sixty minutes. Then stick a toothpick in it when you take it out. If there's bread on it, it's not done. If there's not bread on it, it is done. Cool on a wire rack.

Baked Apple

First, you take an apple and put a hole in it. Then you put raisins in the hole and then put butter over it and then put it in the oven. Then it's done. It tastes delicious!

Popcorn

Put oil and popcorn seeds in a popcorn popper. Then it pops and goes into the bowl. Put some salt on it.

Popsicles

Take a Popsicle set and put juice in part of it. Then freeze them in the freezer. Then you take them out and put them under hot water. Then pull it, and it will open. Then eat it.

Chocolate Chip Cookies

Use Bisquick mix. Cut it into small pieces. You wait until the oven is hot enough. Cook them.

CHAPTER 22

Our Dads Are the Best!

For Father's Day, we make books for fathers telling why they are special. The children dictate their stories to me. Sometimes we write and illustrate books that tell how their dads do things around the house. Here are some of the students' stories

"My dad is the best driver because he knows how to drive. He never drives too slow or too fast, but medium. He is a better driver than my mom, because sometimes she gets past a red light, and she's had accidents some of the time. Now she stops getting in accidents because she listens to the red lights and signs. My dad only goes on green lights. He also wears his seatbelt all the time. Mom does too. Somebody keeps stealing his radio from the truck, three times. He bought a new one that will be stolen no more. He takes it in the house. If they break the glass and see it's gone, they go to another car to steal their radio. That's all I remember."

"My dad cooks the best ribs in the world. First, he buys it at the store. He buys barbecue sauce, chips, hot dogs, hamburgers, and he buys mayonnaise for the egg salad. He buys chicken wings. He also buys soda, and the soda is Fresca and Coke. The he does the dishes and vacuums, with my mom, before he cooks. He puts the ribs on the grill and pours sauce on them. Then he puts the cover down and they start to cook. He checks them every once in a while. After they're done, all the guests are here, and all the kids go play for a little while, and the adults sit around and talk. Then we all eat! My daddy is special!"

"If I break a toy, like a character toy, my dad doesn't get mad at me—like a Jurassic Park or Ghostbusters toy. My brother and I had a pillow fight in the basement, and my brother threw a pillow, which broke a half a leg off the lamp. He didn't get mad, just a little. My dad was fixing somebody else's TV, and I was playing with it and broke the antenna. He went out and bought a new one and didn't get mad. Something he doesn't know about is that when I ride my bike, I sometimes scratch their cars, both of them. I think when he finds this out, he will get mad!"

"I have a chemistry set, which I got for Christmas, or my birthday; I forget which one. It's a real chemistry set that has toys and certain pill things that can hurt you if you handle them wrong or eat them, so I keep it on top of my closet. My dad helps me with the experiments that might hurt me. He mostly does the things and throws the tablets in the water. It's not exactly water but purplish stuff. One experiment was with purple ink. He does all the dangerous stuff so I won't get hurt. Thank you, Dad!"

"My dad is special because he buys me games. He gives me new toys. He tickles me a lot, and I was laughing. In the basement, I laughed when he was talking to my mom. He buys me a new bike because my other bike got broken. He buys me Yu-Gi-Oh cards. He takes me to the park. He takes me to the farm. He knows all about equal and take-away. He is good at math. He is so special every time. I love my dad."

"My dad is special because he comes to school and volunteers. He takes me to Red Lobster. He takes me to the park and cooks me corn on the cob. He takes me to Silver Diner. They have good clams. He cooks me shrimp. He helps me with my homework that I miss at school. He takes me outside to play. He takes me to the doctor when I am sick. He buys me school supplies."

"My dad is the bestest dad on earth. He helps me do my homework. He cooks the food with me. He is the best. I love my dad."

"My dad is special because he loves me. He gives me money. He takes me out to eat. He is nice to me. He lets me sleep in the bed with him when I am scared. He buys me toys. He bought me a bike. He plays with me and my baby sister. He takes us outside. He bought us a brand-new dog. He quit his job and went to another job. I love my dad."

CHAPTER 23

My Dad Can Do Everything!

W e also make handyman books for dads. Perhaps you dads who are reading this book can follow some of their instructions!

How to Mow the Grass

Dad takes the lawn mower out of the garage. Then he fills it up with gas. He lets me start it up. Then he lets me mow the grass, and he does some of it. When he is done, we play soccer.

My dad gets the lawn mower out of the backyard. He pulls the crank to start it. He lawn-mowers the grass. Don't go curved, go straight. Then he stops the lawn mower and puts it back in the back and does the flowers. He takes the rocks out and puts wood chips in them. He puts the flowers inside the ground. He bought some lights and put them underground and plugged them up. Then he throws the rest of the dirt in the garbage because he doesn't need it.

How to Clean a Boat

First, get some cleaning stuff. Then get rags and water. Then you just wash it.

How to Wash the Car

First, have lunch. Then go in the thing that washes the car. Then go fishing.

How to Put Gravel Down

First, my dad gets a shovel. Then he picks up the shovel and he gets the shovel and the gravel. Then he puts the gravel in the wheelbarrow. Then he puts the wheelbarrow down on the ground, and one more thing to do is to do it all over again seventeen times.

How to Work on a Farm

My grandpa shoots deer and chickens so we can eat them. He feeds all the animals water. He feeds the baby horses. He locks them in the barn so they will be in their little stalls so he can feed them. Then he lets them go out and play.

How to Add On to the House

Find someone in the telephone book. Call them and ask if you can add on to your house. Tell them when you want them to come over and then tell them how to do it on a piece of paper. Then you can watch them to see if they do it right.

How to Fix the Rocker

First, my dad takes the hammer and hits the arm part. Then he fixes the seat so we can sit in it because it broke. He adjusted it with a screwdriver. When I was two years old and my grandma sat down in it to rock me, the chair broke. He took it to a couple fix-it shops, and no one could fix it.

How My Dad Washes Clothes

First, my dad takes all the dirty clothes down to the basement and puts them in the washing machine. Then he puts soap in the washing machine. Then he shuts the lid and starts it up. Then he goes upstairs and waits until they're ready to take out and then he puts them in the dryer, and he waits until they are ready to come out and then he takes them out and folds them and then I take them upstairs and put them in my drawers.

How to Paint the House

First, he gets the paint. Then he gets a giant paintbrush. He opens the paint. He tells me and my brother to get out of the house so we won't get in the way. Then he paints the house.

How My Dad Heals People

Yesterday, I hurt my head. My dad kissed it so it would feel better. My dad works in a hospital, and he helps people there. My dad gives me a kiss when I'm not feeling very good. My dad loves me. He helped me when I fell down one time. My dad healed a person. He put his hand on the person's forehead and then he prayed. My dad hurt his leg in Richmond and had to go to the hospital. He almost had to have a cast. He had an X-ray, but it wasn't broken. He dropped wood on his leg.

How to Plan a Trip to Disney World

First, save up the money. Make reservations at a motel. Pack. Start the trip at 6:00 a.m. Stop at a hotel in Georgia near a bridge. Get there the next day. Unpack. Put up the tent in the rain. Look at the stores and everything. Play the video games. Go to the pool with the slide and video games. Play the video games at Disney World. Go to Mickey's Hawaiian Revue at the Magic Kingdom. Watch people playing video games. Pack up again. Take sister to the video games. Take down the tent. Start the journey back home. Get home Sunday, May 28, 1989, at 11:30.

How to Sit and Read the Paper and Help Mom Cook Dinner

My dad sits down by the light and reads the paper. My dad makes red beans and rice. He saves up the ham that we ate yesterday or the day before. He takes red beans and cooks with rice and ham.

How to Cook Hot Dogs and Move

First, my dad takes the hot dogs out of the square thing (refrigerator) and then he puts them in the pan. He turns on the gas stove. Then they're done. After that, he cooks some chili. Then he puts them on a plate and eats them. When we move, he rents a truck. Then he packs all our stuff on the truck and then he takes it away to the new house.

How to Wash the Dishes

He turns on the water. He gets the rag ready to dry the dishes. Then he starts washing them. And then Mom comes home, and she sees the dishes sparkling! And then the kids have to go to bed.

How to Lie Down on the Couch

First, my dad walks to the couch. Then he lays down like this (with his hands behind his head). Then he tries to go to sleep while he watches TV.

How to Fix a Broken Wall

Go to the store with wood in it. Get a piece of wood. Come home. Cut out the shape that can fix the broken part of the wall. Then put plaster on it. Then paint it and let it set for a whole day and a night.

How to Babysit on Saturday

First, my dad cooks breakfast. Then he lets us go out and play. He makes us lunch. He lets my friends come over. Then Mom comes home. He's a good babysitter. He hollers at us only when we are bad!

How to Watch TV

First lay down on the couch. Watch TV. Get some potato chips and eat them. Fall asleep.

My dad sits down and turns on the television. Sometimes he plays on the computer. He goes to bed for a while. My mom tells him that he has to wake up and play with us. Then he goes to work.

How to Clean the House

My dad washes the dishes. He plays with me. He plays on the computer. He uses the vacuum cleaner. He cleans the house. He watches TV and takes a nap. He eats snacks. He plays games.

How to Drink Coffee

My dad puts some coffee seeds in the cup. He puts in water. He cooks it. He puts in milk and sugar. He drinks it. He watches TV. My brother watches TV with him.

How My Dad Gets Angry

There are these kids playing soccer near my dad's two cars, and they kick the ball on our two cars. My dad gets the ball and keeps it for twenty seconds. My dad asks them why they can't go up to the other street. They say their mothers won't let them.

CHAPTER 24

How Should I Take Care of a Baby?

O ne year, one of our teachers was pregnant with twins. Shortly before the babies were due to arrive, my students wrote a handbook for her, instructing her on how to care for her babies. Here are some of their instructions, in the words that they used to dictate their stories to me.

How to Change a Diaper

You know the side where the tape is. Take the tape off of the side. Then take the diaper off. Then kind of put the diaper like that. [Here he drew a triangle shape.] Then pick it up and hold it together in one or two hands. Put it in the trash can. Then get a new diaper. Put the baby's legs up. Put the diaper underneath. Then find the tape and put the other side of the tape together.

Get a diaper. Get some tissues. Wet the tissues with warm water. Or get a Baby Fresh Wipes. Take off the dirty diaper. Wipe the baby. Put on a clean diaper. Put the powder on. Stripe the diaper with the side things.

First take off his old diaper. Get a new diaper. Get some baby oil. Put the oil on the diaper. Put the diaper on the baby. Put the baby to bed, and he goes again. Do everything all over again.

First, you take off the diaper. Then you wipe the baby's bottom. Then you put another diaper on. The baby can go now.

Buy a pack of diapers. Take off the dirty one. Throw it away. Clean his bottom. Put some baby powder on it. Put the diaper on.

Pull off his pants. Take off his socks and shoes. Then you grab his legs. Then you take the wipes and wipe his bottom. If that doesn't work, put baby powder on. Then you unfold the diaper and put it under his bottom. Then you fold the diaper up. Then you strap it on with little strips. Then put his pants and socks and shoes back on.

How to Dress a Baby

First, you put the baby in some clothes. Then you put on its pants, then its shirt. Maybe one day you would like to dress it in a dress. After you have dressed it, you take it anywhere you'd like, or you can stay home. Then, when it's time for the baby to go to bed, you put it in its nightgown. First, you put the bottom of the nightgown on it. Then you put the top of it on. When it's all ready, you sing a song to it or maybe read to it. Then you tuck it in, and you say, "Good night," and then it falls asleep. Then the next day, you get it up, but not too early in the morning, and you do it all over again.

How to Give a Baby a Bath

Take off the baby's clothes. Put the baby in the special thing in the sink or tub. Get baby shampoo in the hair, but make sure it doesn't get in the eyes. Clean the baby's toes. Put the water on warm. Take the baby out, and put its pajamas on.

How to Put a Baby to Sleep

Read the longest book you can. Read it to the baby. If he starts crying, put him on his back.

Take a big book. Read it. Do what the book says. Take some sleeping gas. Put the baby to sleep with it.

First, you rock it to sleep. You sing a lullaby. You put him down in the bed. It goes to sleep.

Get a rocking chair. Get the babies. Then rock them. And give them their bottles. Then they'll go to sleep.

Put the baby in its crib. Rock it, and at the same time, sing a lullaby. Give it its teddy bear.

You pick up the baby. Swing it in your arms. Put it in the crib.

I would sing a soft lullaby quietly. I would give it a little bear. Then I would turn on some little baby music. If she still doesn't go to sleep (or he), I would sit in the rocking chair and hold both of the babies and rock them to sleep.

Put the baby in his crib. Say, "Good night." Sing a lullaby.

How to Feed the Baby

First, you get baby food. Then you get a spoon. Then you open the baby food up. Then you feed it. Then you burp it. Then you give it a bottle.

Get a bottle. Put a little bit of milk in it. Warm it up. Hold the baby in your arms. Put the bottle in the baby's mouth. Don't push too hard, because if you push too hard, it would choke.

Get some formula. Put it in the bottle. Put it in the microwave to get it warm. Get the baby. See if the formula is too hot. Feed it.

You take a baby spoon. Go to the store. Buy baby food. Put it in the mouth.

First, you go to the store. Buy five hundred cans of baby food. Then you get one of the baby food jars. Get a baby spoon. Put the baby spoon in the baby food. Get the baby. Tell her if she doesn't eat, she'll starve. Stuff it in her mouth.

You have to get the bottle and put it in the plastic. Then you put the milk in. You put it in the refrigerator. When the baby starts crying, get the bottle, and put it in the microwave, and heat it up. Then you give it to the baby. Then you hold him until he goes to sleep. You put him in his crib and then he goes to sleep in his crib.

How to Burp a Baby

Pick up the baby. Put the baby on your shoulder. Pat the baby's back. It will burp.

Turn the baby on its tummy. Hit it on the back lightly. It burps.

First, you feed it. Then you put the baby halfway over your shoulder. Then you hit its back softly. Then it burps.

How to Babysit

Put the baby in the crib. If it cries, give it a bottle. If it gets its diaper wet, change it.

How to Make a Baby Laugh

Make funny faces. If that doesn't work, put your head in her stomach and turn it around. If that doesn't work, get laughing gas.

How to Take Care of a Baby

You clean it and you feed it and you burp it and you keep it away from things that will hurt it. Keep it from doing things that can harm it.

CHAPTER 25

I Can't Wait until Graduation Day!

For many years, I have had my students make time capsules that are not to be opened until high school graduation day. A letter is sent home to the parents explaining the project, and each child is asked to bring to school a shoe box wrapped in paper so that the lid can be removed. Parents are to write a letter that they would like for their child to read on graduation day and put it in a sealed envelope inside the capsule. At school, we do several activities to make things to enclose in the box, which include

- making a list of favorite things, such as movies, TV programs, stories, games, and food;
- tracing their hand and foot;

- measuring their height with a piece of string, which is then wrapped around a strip of card stock that says, "This is how tall I am in first grade";
- drawing a picture of how they look in first grade and how they think they will look when they graduate; and
- writing about what they want to do when they grow up.

I include in each capsule a class picture, an individual picture of each child doing an activity in school, and a personal letter including reminders of special things each student did during the year. I also include my phone number and address, requesting that they contact me when they graduate. We make a big deal of sealing the capsules securely with tape and then tying the boxes with string to deter the children from opening them before graduation day.

I had a phone call one year from a young man living in Kentucky who had graduated the day before and had just opened his time capsule. He told me that his capsule had been to several foreign countries, as his father had moved several times with his job assignments and was now stationed in Kentucky. We had a wonderful conversation! I was invited to the graduation party of another young man, and the highlight of the party was to watch him open his capsule and measure his hand, foot, and height against what they had been in first grade! And then there was another child who told me, the day after he took his time capsule home, that he couldn't wait and opened it right away! Another told me that he put his capsule in a special place, way up high so that no one could get to it. I have met others over the years who have said that they were eagerly awaiting the time that they graduated so they could open their time capsules.

Just today, while I was completing work on this book, I received a letter in the mail from a former student who is in college now. She wrote a very interesting letter telling me about what has transpired in her life since first grade. Her letter says, "I will always remember how excited I was to open up my time capsule. I constantly felt like the day would never come! I excitedly opened the box the day of graduation at my party with my family. My relatives couldn't believe that I had held on to it that long (even through two moves), and they were astounded by even the idea. I wanted to personally thank you for allowing me to have that opportunity to create something that I will cherish for years to come."

CHAPTER 26

Dear Mrs. Fizer

Over the years, I have received some very interesting letters from students and parents. Here are some of them, in their own words—and some in their own spelling and punctuation!

Dear mrs. fizer
I Will miss you this summer may I have my Toy back

To Mrs. Fizer,
You are the Qeen of the world. Because you are nise. I love you mrs fizer. With you I would be happy I like you miss Fizer. Have a nice day thank you miss Fizer. I will miss you.

Dear Mrs Fizer

I hope you are very good to your kids.

So far you have been one of the best teachers ever, Mrs. Fizer, sometimes the work you give me is hard, but then again you give me easy homework. I will miss you Mrs. Fizer. I'll visit you. Bye!
Your best student,

Dear Mrs. Fizer
I love you. I am sad because school is over. I love school. I hate when school is over. Let me know when my summer homework is ready. Will it be ready today? It has to be ready by all summer. P.S. I hope you think of me more then any class or student.
Love,

Dear Miss Firss
You are not juss My tetchr you are my Friend and thing you for teching me my mom seid she like you ais my tetch and I do to.

Dear mrs fizer, am I dowen good on my riyport coad write me bck plese

Mrs. Fizer
I liked having yu for a 1st grade Techer this year. I hope you enjoy the sumer You have put a lot of learning in me. You're a great teacher for me!!

I love miss fossil. You are The Best teach thay I have. These are my brother name are cory and Herman

Dear Miss fizer
I have missed you so so so much it has been great in 2 grad so you stell have Super Kids I will see you love. I still love first grad! I miss you very bad I have been sad I don't see you very much

Dear Ms Fizer
How are you? My sisters saw you at gint when they were sick One went to the hospital how was everything did you injoy your summer ms. Fizer you are the best techer in the wold are you injoying the fall and October?

Dear Ms. Fizer,
I'm glad you were my teacher. You taught me how to read. I think you were the one who really got me in START (a program for gifted students). You taught me everything I need to know. Now I'm sitting here in third grade doing work that you taught me. I'd love to go back in your class. You were a great teacher. I'll miss you when I move to Middle School.
Love,

To Mrs Fizer
Hello I hope you're fine. I want to thank you for the birthday card you sent me it was nice thank you so much. Here are some pioctres for you and Mr. Fizer. Hope to see you soon.

One child made a beautiful card for me with the following written inside: "An apple a day keeps the teacher away. You're being a great teacher."

Notes from parents were usually short and to the point. But occasionally, I received one that said much more.

From a parent from another country:
Dear Mrs. Fizer,
With due respect, is it possible that for Tuesday, Nov. 26, school bus pick my child up from day care in the morning instead of her regular bus stop because I have some work to do so I will drop her in day care in the morning. I want that school bus will pick her from there after school. She always goes to day care. I will tell at the day care that tomorrow she is going to school from here. If it is possible, please let me know. Her day care is _____ and address us _____ and phone number is _____. I will be very thankful to you.

A father who didn't have time to listen to his child read one evening wrote this:
Dear Mrs. Fizer,
Tonight I cooked a porterhouse steak surrounded with twenty-eight mushrooms stuffed with shrimp for my lovely, overworked wife. Thursday I have back-to-school night at my school. Is it possible for my son to bring home his reading book Friday so he and I will have time to go over it?
PS—I am giving my son penmanship lessons patterned after my style of writing. Now tell me, ain't it successful!

CHAPTER 27

Don't Have Any More Babies!

On my birthday in November 2006, I walked into my school and decided that it was time for me to retire, so I went to the classroom, dropped off my belongings, returned to the office, and announced to the principal that I would be retiring at the end of the school year.

He looked at me in surprise and asked, "Is it because of something that I have done?" (This was his first year as principal in the school.)

I assured him that it was not anything that he had done but that I just thought it was time to retire.

Once the children at school heard that I would not be returning the next year, they began to ask me why I wanted to leave. One child who had been in my class the previous year came to me one morning, gave me a hug, and said, "Mrs. Fizer, you can't retire."

I proceeded to tell him several reasons I had for retiring, and he responded, "But, Mrs. Fizer, if you retire, you will have to move to a retirement home!"

Another child asked me why I wanted to retire, and I answered with a question, "Why do you think I would want to retire?"

His response was, "So you can be an old lady!"

Often, during summer break, I help to teach Vacation Bible School at my church. Some of the children who go to the school where I teach attend this Bible School. A neighbor to some of these children asked two of the boys if they were going to attend VBS one summer, and one asked, "Is Mrs. Fizer going to be there?"

The other replied, "No, she just retired!"

I was having a conference with the parents of one of my students shortly before I retired. At the end of the conference, the mother, who was older when she had her son who was in my class (she also had two sons in their late teens), commented that she had heard that I was retiring and that she had to give me some advice. Her advice was, "Please don't have any more babies!"

I am really enjoying my retirement, although I miss the children. I am fortunate to have several children living nearby, and I have helped some of them with homework, listened to them read, or helped them to write their name correctly. I also am the accompanist for the children's choir at church, and I am so pleased when some of the children run up to me at church and give me a big hug. I especially enjoy spending time with my two grandchildren, ages six and fourteen, and following their progress through their education. I am very pleased that they, and their mother, agreed to be the illustrators for my book!

CHAPTER 28

Miscellaneous

Some of the more interesting things that happen in the classroom do not fit in with any specific academic area but make a teacher's day so much more fun and interesting. I have included some of these things in this miscellaneous category.

One spring day, the children were arriving at school in a downpour of rain after a night of heavy rains and flooding in some areas. Arthur came in, dripping wet, and said, "Mrs. Fizer, this is the worstest day of my life."

Jerome came in just as wet as Arthur and said, "Mrs. Fizer, it is raining outside!"

My students enjoyed running laps around the soccer field at recess time. Stacy came to me one day and said, "Mrs. Fizer, may I run laptops around the soccer field today?"

Billy, who came from a single-mom home, came in one morning and very excitedly told me that his mom had tucked him and his sister in bed earlier than usual and she had on a beautiful nightgown because her boyfriend was coming over!

Patsy asked me one day, "Mrs. Fizer, why don't you work?"

Before prayer was not allowed in schools, my students and I always said grace before going to lunch. One day, the mother of one of my students came to me and asked that we stop saying grace because her daughter was getting confused with what to say at home when they said grace. I told her that we would continue to say grace and that her daughter could bow her head along with the rest of the students but not say anything. The mother agreed, so I told her daughter the next morning what she could do during our grace time. After a few days, she was saying grace along with the rest of the class, and I heard nothing else about it from the mother. If I had done this in my later years of teaching, I would probably have been fired!

After the terrible tsunami in Indonesia, our school decided to collect coins for relief there. Each class was provided with a small plastic bucket in which the children were to put their coins each day, if they chose to do so. On the day that this project was explained to the class, Richard was absent. Upon his return the next day, children were gathered around the bucket, dropping in their coins. He asked what they were doing, and one of the girls said, "We are collecting coins for *salami*!"

Our entire school was transferred to a new building one year, with all new equipment! It was very exciting to be in the new facility with all this modern equipment—until I wanted to play a cassette in my new boom box. This was the year that the Macarena dance was very popular, and I was going to have the children get their exercise by dancing this dance. I tried and tried to get the cassette to play, and, no matter what I did, nothing worked.

Finally Karen came to my rescue and said, "Mrs. Fizer, if you would turn on the power, the tape would play!"

And, with a very red face, I pushed the power button, and we danced the Macarena!

I was teaching when schools first became integrated, and I had only one African American child in my classroom that first year. For some reason that I have never understood, that particular year, students could order ice cream, and it was delivered to the classroom after lunch. The students who ordered the ice cream ate it while the others continued with whatever they were doing at the time. I always made a list of who ordered the ice cream and, when it was delivered to the classroom, let those who ordered get it themselves, without making a big deal of passing it out.

For several days, we came up with one ice cream missing, so I decided to check closely to see what was going on. I found that the African American child was eating ice cream but had not ordered any, so I questioned him about it. He said that he wanted some ice cream, so he took it because his mom wouldn't let him buy it.

I felt that I needed to let his parents know about this, so I sent a note home. That night, we had a PTA meeting, and one of the first persons I saw there was his mother, coming down the hallway toward me. I had all kinds of thoughts running through my mind, wondering whether she would accuse me of blaming him because he was black.

She approached me and said, "Mrs. Fizer, thank you for the note my son brought home today. I decided that if he wanted ice cream, that he should have ice cream, so I went to the store and bought a half gallon and made him eat it all. I don't think he will ever take anyone else's ice cream again."

And he never did!

I was having a conference after school one day and heard a voice calling from the restroom in the corner of the classroom, "Mrs. Fizer, will you come and wipe my hiney?" I was very surprised because all the students were supposed to be gone for the day, so I checked the restroom. One of my boys was there. He had missed his bus because he was in the restroom waiting for me to wipe his hiney!

Carlos came to me, very upset, one day and said that another of the boys had said a very bad word that only adults are allowed to say!

Jonah told me one day that he was a baby when he was fifteen years old and that he had very cute hair!

Kimberly, after having her grandmother visit her, came to school one day and said, "I never want to get old, because then you get all short and shriveled."

As the class was working quietly one day, we suddenly heard the shrill sound of a whistle blowing in the classroom. I asked who had a whistle and blew it, and Amber reluctantly said, "It is my whistle." I then asked her why she would blow it in the classroom, and she said, "I just wanted to see if it would work!"

One day, we were preparing for a tornado drill in our school. As I was preparing for the drill and explaining to the children what they should do when the drill began, Sierra asked, "If we do a good job, will we get ice cream?"

Dylan went into the classroom restroom and locked the door, as the children usually do when they go there. When he was ready to come out, he couldn't get the door unlocked. He called out to tell me that he couldn't open the door. I gave him several suggestions, and none worked, so I called the office to tell them our problem and get help. Luckily, maintenance men were in the building at that time and were sent to the room to help. As they were trying to determine how to get the door opened, Dylan called out, "Do you want me to turn out the light to save energy?" (This was during the time of President Johnson's energy-saving days.) The workers finally had to go through the ceiling to get the door opened from the inside, and they found Dylan standing in the very dark restroom, patiently waiting!

Toward the end of the school year, some of the children had slacked off in completing their work. Having them work during recess had not helped, so I told three students that they couldn't go home until their work was finished They continued to waste time, so, when time came to pack up to go home, I would not let them get ready, but I told them to keep working. They continued to waste time! When the first graders were dismissed to go to the buses, I sent the other children out and would not let these three go.

Henry got busy and finished right away, and he got to leave.

Mikey and Andy started crying and saying that they had to leave because the buses would go without them. I knew that I had about ten minutes' leeway before they would miss their buses because the students were dismissed by grade level.

Mikey started crying loudly, saying, "I need help! Please help me!"

I told him that he should have finished his work earlier, that I could have helped him then, but it was now past 3:30, and I did not have to work past 3:30, so I couldn't help him. Surprisingly, he finished in about two minutes and got to leave.

Andy was sobbing, saying, "My parents will kill me if I am not on the bus. They will come looking for me, and when they find me, they will kill me." He didn't quite get finished, but I did let him go anyway so he wouldn't get killed! Their work habits improved immensely the next day!

On Sundays, I am the organist for my church. On one particular Sunday, one of my students, Emma, came to church with her grandmother. She was very surprised when she came to the front of the church for the children's story to see me at the organ, and she kept waving to me. The children were dismissed to go to their classes, and she got all the way to the back of the sanctuary and then came running back down the aisle, saying, "I can't leave until I give Mrs. Fizer a hug." She ran all the way to the organ, gave me a big hug, and proceeded on her way!

While I was sitting on the playground bench one day, three of my girls came to sit with me. What a conversation we had! Jenny said, "You're old, Mrs. Fizer."

I asked her why she thought so, and she said, "You have little white things in your hair, and you are short and you wear glasses. You wear tennis shoes all the time. You have something hanging under your chin."

I asked her what I could do to look younger, and all three volunteered information.

"You can wear a dress." (I almost always wear slacks.)

"You can eat lunch with us." (I still haven't figured out how this would make me look younger!)

"You can wear sandals."

"You can go to KC's Beauty Mart and get some extensions for your hair."

A few days later, I did wear a dress and sandals to school, put on more makeup than I normally wore, and borrowed a long, dark wig from a coworker, which I put on while they were in the library. What fun we had when they returned to class and saw me with my new look!

At some point in my career, we began having parent conferences with all parents, not just when there was a problem. Beth's mother came in for her scheduled conference and sat wringing her hands all the way through, saying that she had never had to come to a conference with a teacher before and was so nervous she didn't know what to do or say. Fortunately, I had nothing but good things to say about her daughter!

I have a black shirt with white spots on it that I wear quite often because it is very comfortable. One day, Stephanie, who had been in my class the year before, saw me in the hall and asked, "Mrs. Fizer, when are you going to wear your journal shirt again?" My shirt reminded her of the black–and-white marble composition books that we write in. So now, anytime I wear that shirt, I look her up and tell her that I am wearing my journal shirt.

I have another shirt with dogwood flowers on it. Devon, in another class, remarked that she liked my state-flower shirt. (The dogwood is the state flower of Virginia.)

The school secretary appeared at my door one morning, just after school had begun, and asked to see Judy with her backpack. I had no idea why, but I sent Judy to the hallway with the backpack. After looking through the backpack and talking with her, the secretary told me that Judy's mom had called to ask if she would check the backpack because their hamster was missing, and she suspected that her daughter had put the hamster in her backpack and brought it to school because she had asked to do so and was disappointed when she was told that she couldn't do it. The secretary asked Judy about it. Judy replied that she had indeed brought the hamster to school in her backpack and then let a fifth-grade friend take the hamster to her classroom because they had a cage in their classroom that the hamster could stay in for the day. The mom was called and came to school to retrieve the hamster!

Another mom came to the classroom soon after classes had begun one day and asked to speak to her son. He went into the hallway to see her and then came back into the classroom, got his backpack, and went back out. A minute or two later, the mom came into the room with him, thanked me for letting her see him, and said that he had picked up her wedding ring from the counter when she had removed it to wash her hands and brought it to school to give to his girlfriend! When she couldn't find it at home, she suspected that he may have taken it because he had been talking about his girlfriend!

One of my energetic boys, Gary, was dancing around as we walked down the hall in line to go to lunch. I asked him to show me the right way to walk in line, and he walked very straight, with his hands by his sides. I complimented him and told him that he looked like a handsome young man walking like that. Seconds later, he was doing his dance again, and I asked him what happened to the handsome young man walking correctly. Gary replied, "I am walking like this because I want to be a kid, not a young man!"

One of the girls in my class arrived one morning wearing a new raincoat. I commented on how pretty it was, and she spun around, as if modeling, and said, "It's a London Fog!"

A student asked one of the other students if she was from China. She replied that she was from Korea, and he told her, "I am from China because I eat Chinese food."

Our speech teacher appeared at my door on the first day of school with a first grader who couldn't find his classroom. She was trying to help him, but she couldn't find his name on any of the six first-grade teachers' class rosters. I asked him what his name was and he replied, "Bill." I said, "What is your last name?" His response—"Doodlebug, Bill Doodlebug. That's what my grandma calls me!"

Gail came up to me and said that she couldn't sit in her chair because her neighbor had put glue on the seat. I questioned the culprit and asked her why she would do such a thing, and she replied, "I just wanted to find out what would happen if she sat down in a chair with glue on it."

Stuart came in one day with both top front teeth missing and two on the bottom also. He smiled a big smile and said, "My mom says that I look just like a pumpkin!"

At sharing time one day, Dewey brought in a picture of him when he was in a wedding as the ring bearer. He explained to the class what he had to do as the ring bearer.

Christopher said, "I was the pillow bearer in a wedding one time too."

I sent Lee and Emma to take some posters to the library to be laminated one day and asked them to repeat to me what they were to tell the librarian: "Please laminate these for Mrs. Fizer."

They said to me, "Please eliminate these for Mrs. Fizer."

My second year of teaching, I had a class of seventh graders, which at that time was the highest grade in an elementary school. One of the students was a beautiful blonde girl who was not the least bit interested in school. One day, during a discussion, I asked a question, and her hand went up very quickly. I was so excited that she was paying attention and had volunteered to answer, so I called on her. She said, "Mrs. Fizer, what color is your lipstick?"

Norma arrived a few minutes late one morning, opened the door, and announced to the class, in a very loud voice, "Hello, people, I'm here."

I was calling on children in the class to answer questions one day and had not called on Andrew yet. I suppose he got tired of waiting, because he shouted out, "Hello, you haven't called me yet!"

I was sitting on the playground bench at recess one day when two girls from another first-grade class came up and sat with me. We were talking about various things, and then one of the girls said, "Look, we are twins. We all have on blue and white." I told her that twins means two people and that there were three of us sitting there, so we must be triplets, not twins, because triplet means three. A few minutes later, another child walked up, and the student said to her, "Look, we all have on blue and white. We are piglets."

Matthew was passing out cookies with frosting at snack time one day. I noticed that, as he handed each child a cookie, he licked his fingers before handing out the next one. I suggested that he should not lick his fingers, that it was not healthy to lick your fingers and then touch food being given to others, and he replied, "But I am licking my fingers after I pass out a cookie, not before I pick up the next one!"

I must include one story about my grandson, which he told me when he had just completed first grade. We were at the beach, and he made friends with a girl playing in the sand near us while his mother, my daughter, was talking with the little girl's mom. Later, when we were back at our cottage, my daughter told us that the little girl and her mom were visiting her parents who lived at the beach and that they lived in Texas. My grandson, who was listening to our conversation, said, "Texas! That is where my teacher used to live. Then she moved to America and came to teach at my school!"

BIOGRAPHY

I grew up in a very small coal-mining town in southern West Virginia and always thought that my teachers were the most wonderful people in the world. I wanted to be just like them when I grew up. I graduated from Northfork High School and from Concord College in Athens, West Virginia, where I earned a BS degree in elementary education. I then earned my master's degree at George Mason University in Fairfax, Virginia. I have lived in Woodbridge, Virgnia, just a short distance from Washington, DC, for fifty years with my husband, to whom I have been married for fifty-five years.

We have three children and two grandchildren, who are the lights of our lives!